Lynne Farris

A Touch of Felt

- 22 Fresh & Fun Projects
- Stylish Gifts & Designer Accents
- Inventive Needle Felting & Appliqué

C&T PUBLISHING

Text copyright © 2009 by Lynne Farris

Artwork copyright © 2009 by C&T Publishing, Inc.

Publisher: AMY MARSON

Creative Director: GAILEN RUNGE

Acquisitions Editor: JAN GRIGSBY

Editor: LYNN KOOLISH

Technical Editors: CAROL ZENTGRAF AND TERESA STROIN

Copyeditor/Proofreader: WORDFIRM INC.

Cover Designer/Book Designer: KRISTEN YENCHE

Production Coordinator: TIM MANIBUSAN

Illustrator: GREGG VALLEY

Photography by LUKE MULKS, DIANE PEDERSEN, AND CHRISTINA
CARTY-FRANCIS of C&T Publishing unless otherwise noted

Furniture provided by GRANGEWOOD ANTIQUES

Published by C&T Publishing, Inc., P.O. Box 1456, Lafayette, CA 94549

Library of Congress Cataloging-in-Publication Data
Farris, Lynne.
  A touch of felt : 22 fresh & fun projects : stylish gifts & designer
accents : inventive needle felting & appliqué / Lynne Farris.
    p. cm.
  ISBN 978-1-57120-500-1 (paper trade : alk. paper)
 1. Felt work. 2. Felting. 3. House furnishings. I. Title.
TT849.5.F385 2009
  746'.0463--dc22

Printed in China

10 9 8 7 6 5 4 3 2 1

acknowledgments

Once again my friend Mary Woodall and I have proven the old adage that two heads are better than one! We've worked together so well for so long that it's hard to imagine doing a project of this magnitude without her. Mary's nimble fingers and creative genius are evident throughout the projects.

Thanks also to Mary and her husband, Bill, for their fabulous hospitality during our creative extravaganzas at their home in Virginia. Thanks to Lambert Greene for getting me and my studio stuff back and forth to Virginia, and thanks to my brother, Roland Stubblefield, and his wife, Debbie, for continually supporting and encouraging my work.

Thanks to my friends at C&T Publishing, Gailen Runge, Jan Grigsby, Amy Marson, and my editor, Lynn Koolish, for their help in bringing this project to completion. I truly appreciate their willingness to work me into the schedule despite several unexpected challenges and delays this year. Thanks to my good friend Carol Zentgraf for checking all the details and making it all work.

Thanks to all the companies (listed in Sources) that supported the project with products and tools.

Thanks to you, from the bottom of my heart, for your interest in my work and for purchasing this book!

contents

Acknowledgments 3

Introduction 6

Tools and Materials 7

Working with Felt 12

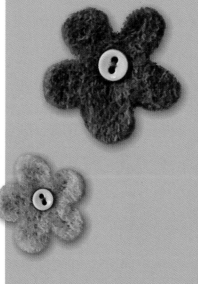

dining in style—
AUTUMN LEAVES ACCENTS

Falling Leaves
Table Runner. 18

Falling Leaves
Placemats 20

Leaves of Gold
Coasters 22

Felted Leaves Napkin Rings
and Votive Covers 24

Stems and Leaves
Centerpiece 26

Layered Felt Vase Wrap . . 29

a place for everything—
ORGANIZING ACCENTS

Desktop Caddy 33

Mosaic Stripes Needle-Felted
Paper Tray 35

Sculpted Felt Pencil Cup...38

Felted Fruits
Decorative Box..................40

Felted Fruits Appliqué
Picture Frame...................42

Needle-Felted
Bookshelf Trim..................45

jewel tones—
CONTEMPORARY
FOLK-ART ACCENTS

Memento Board 48

Four Hearts Pillow 52

Paisley Envelope Pillow . 55

Pursonal Diary Tote. . . . 58

Hearts and Flowers
Footstool 61

tranquil bedroom—
ROSE GARDEN ACCENTS

Dream Keeper Pillow 65

Dream Journal Cover 68

Still Life with Roses 70

Bed of Roses
Sheer Bed Scarf. 73

Rose Garden
Curtain Tiebacks 76

Sources 78

About the Author 79

introduction

I've been creating with fabric for about as long as I can remember. It all started with my grandmother, Adele McBurney Stubblefield, an incredibly talented, creative, and resourceful woman who spent most of every day involved in some aspect of a sewing or needlework project. She made intricate patchwork quilts, crochet bedspreads, cutwork tablecloths, tatting for pillowcases, and all the special-occasion dresses my sister and I wore throughout our early childhood. Sometimes she took me on exciting field trips to the fabric section of the Main Street department store in my hometown. We'd look at all the newest pattern books, touch all the fabrics, and pick through the buttons and notions to select the perfect ones to begin a new project. Other times she'd use whatever fabric she had available at home, perhaps even one of her old gabardine coats, and through her own ingenuity, no patterns required, she would restyle the fabric into the most adorable little handmade outfits for me and my sister.

My big sister, Diane, and I in our handmade Easter outfits, circa 1951

During the countless hours I spent perched by my grandmother's side, she would stop patiently to give me scraps of fabric to play with and encourage me to create for my little dolls miniature versions of the clothes she was making for us. Those magical hours of fun and the gift of patient attention from my grandmother instilled in me a love of fabric, color, and texture, a confidence in my own creative instincts, and the curiosity to pursue fabric art throughout a satisfying and multifaceted career as a teacher, designer, author, and artist.

Over the past several years, my creative attention has been focused on working with wool felt, concentrating on various techniques of felt sculpture, felt appliqué, and needle felting. Wool felt is a truly versatile material with luscious colors and textures; it's easy to use, and it provides endless opportunities for manipulation and embellishment. It can be used to create a variety of looks from contemporary to traditional.

I've designed this collection of projects to showcase numerous felting and appliqué techniques. My goal is to inspire you to express your own creativity through the medium of felt. I encourage you to read through the first two chapters, which cover felt tips and techniques and tools and materials, before you embark on any of the projects. You'll find some great shortcuts, new tools, and new approaches that will ensure your success.

The projects shown here can easily be adapted to suit your own style and color preferences. Complete full-size patterns and fully illustrated step-by-step instructions are included for each of the 22 projects. The bonus is that as you try the different techniques, you'll end up with great gifts for your friends and family and beautiful decorative accents to use throughout your home.

Feast your eyes, feed your soul, and feather your nest! Happy felting!

—Lynne Farris

tools and materials

Wool

Woven wool and wool felt come in a variety of widths, ranging from 36˝ to 72˝ wide. Wool felt is also often available in precut squares. Refer to the materials lists to see how much fabric is needed for each project. When a yardage is given (rather than specific dimensions), 36˝-wide fabric is sufficient.

Wool Felt

Wool felt is currently my absolutely favorite fabric! All the projects in this book feature wool felt in the starring role. It has great body and density, so it is easy to work with, doesn't fray, cuts easily, and can be manipulated and embellished to create myriad textures and surface designs.

Wool felt

Felted Wool

Felted woven wool is available commercially in an array of coordinated hand-dyes, plaids, checks, and solids (see Sources on page 78). You can also create your own felted wool by washing woven or knitted wool—technically this process is called fulling (page 14).

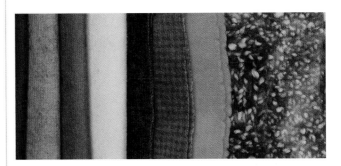

Felted woven and knitted wool

Wool Roving

Wool roving is made of dyed fibers that have been carded to smooth them. It is available in an almost infinite variety of beautiful colors. Needle felt it onto a background fabric as an embellishment, use it as the fiber to hold two layers of fabric together, or start from scratch and create your own fabric by arranging roving layers perpendicular to one another and needle felting them together.

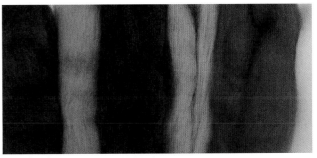

Wool roving

Wool Fleece

Wool fleece is made from wool or wool-blend fibers that have been dyed but not carded. This fluffy fiber is used the same way as roving, but it has just a bit less sheen. It entangles easily, so it is easy to felt.

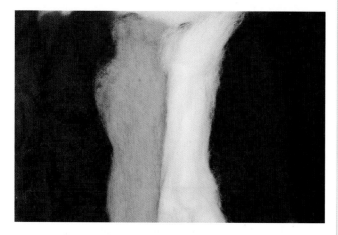

Wool fleece

Silk Hankies

A beautiful way to add sheen, glorious color, and silky highlights to your projects is to use hand-dyed silk hankies for needle felting (see Sources on page 78). Hankies are natural silk fibers that have been spread into a thin layer and then stacked and dyed in a random pattern with a group of related colors. You can pull off small bits of a hankie and stretch them into a very thin web of fibers that can be needle felted onto the surface of your work. Because the silk fibers are so smooth, they don't always attach readily. To ensure that the fibers become entangled permanently, try blending a bit of wool roving in coordinating colors with the silk fibers.

Hand-dyed silk hankies

Specialty Yarns

Yarn is a great material for adding detail, outlines, or texture to a project. It can be needle felted or couched in place. Including yarn in your felting projects is a great way to use yarn scraps from other projects. Several varieties of novelty yarns were used for the projects in this book, including a bold felted roving yarn and an unusually bumpy bouclé (see Sources on page 78).

Novelty yarns

fast2fuse Double-Sided Fusible Stiff Interfacing

Several projects require the support of a stiff interfacing between the layers. Heavyweight fast2fuse offers excellent support and is easy to stitch through. It has fusible adhesive on both sides to make quick work of bonding the layers together. For projects requiring a softer look, you may prefer to simply add another layer of felt between the layers for additional body (see Sources on page 78).

fast2fuse

Simply Stems

The Stems and Leaves centerpiece project on page 26 calls for paper-wrapped wire stems. I recommend Simply Stems; they are strong enough to support the leaves but flexible enough to be shaped into a natural branch-like arch (see Sources on page 78).

Simply Stems

Marking Tools

Most of the projects in this book involve tracing a template and transferring stitching lines to your fabric with some kind of marking tool before you cut or sew. Because you will be stitching directly on the lines, avoid using pencils or permanent inks, which will leave unsightly marks on your project. Instead, use an air- or water-soluble fabric marker for marking lines on light colors, and use a chalk wheel or chalk marking tool for marking on dark colors.

Marking tools

Cutting Tools

Sharp-pointed scissors and a rotary cutter and cutting mat are essential for cutting out sewn shapes accurately. Additionally, some projects call for a rotary blade with a scallop or pinking edge to create a decorative edge. For the reverse appliqué technique, you will need small sharp-pointed scissors, such as embroidery scissors, so that you can cut close to your stitching lines through several layers of felt.

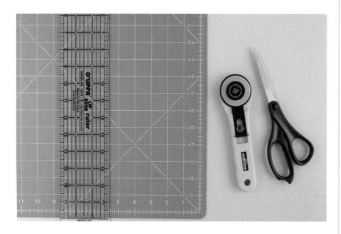

Cutting tools

Adhesives

A few of the projects require specialized adhesives. One of my favorites is a really strong double-sided adhesive called SuperTape. It is available in rolls of various widths as well as in sheets. The sheet form has peel-away paper backing with a transparent covering that allows you to cut it into any shape and then maintain control while applying the adhesive.

Another great fabric glue is Fabri-Tac, a liquid adhesive that is clear, easy to apply, and fast drying. It's available in a bottle with a very small tip for hard to reach areas.

A third and invaluable adhesive tool is Sulky KK2000, a repositionable temporary adhesive spray that lets you arrange your appliqué pieces or felt layers without using bulky straight pins that might distort the shapes as you stitch. You can stitch over this adhesive without damaging your machine or your needle.

Adhesives

Sewing Machine

You will need a sewing machine with a straight stitch and a zigzag stitch, and you'll need the ability to lower the feed dogs for free-motion stitching. An open-toe embroidery foot is really helpful, if available. Before embarking on a new project, treat yourself to a new needle.

You will find that felt generates a fair amount of lint, so clean out the bobbin race and the presser foot assembly regularly to ensure smooth operation. And do yourself a favor—have your machine serviced on a regular basis.

Sewing machine

Felting Tools

Felting Needle

Felting needles are sharp needles about 3½″ long with burrs near one end. When the burred end pierces the fabric, the burrs catch the wool fibers and carry them through the surface, entangling the fibers and felting them together. Use a single needle for detail work, such as yarn outlines, or when felting small areas.

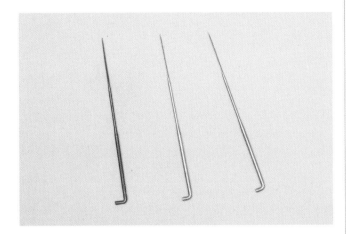

Felting needles

Foam Pad

When needle felting by hand, you must place your work on a 1½″- or 2″-thick foam pad to protect your needles and work surface. Always work on a table or solid surface. NEVER work in your lap.

Needle felt on a foam pad.

Multineedle Felting Tool and Pad

The Clover Felting Needle Tool is a plastic holder that allows you to work with five needles at once. A protective shield moves up and down when the needles are engaged to keep you from accidentally "vaccinating" yourself. You can use the tool with a foam pad or with the special brush pad also available from Clover (see Sources on page 78).

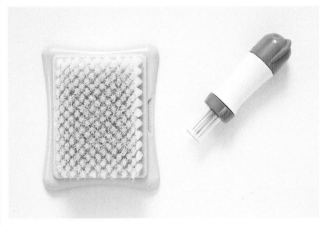

Felting needle tool and brush pad

Embellisher Machine

Baby Lock's Embellisher machine is the ultimate tool for the serious needle felter. Seven needles and quick up-and-down action make quick work of needle felting a large surface. You can remove the needles individually and use only one or two for detail work, felting yarns in place, and felting in tight spots (see Sources on page 78).

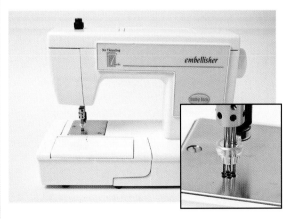

Embellisher machine

working with felt

For a thorough understanding of the techniques used in this book, read this section before you embark on the projects. You'll find that these shortcuts and simplified methods will free you to express your creative side while avoiding the tedium of more-complicated traditional sewing and felting techniques.

Making and Using Pattern Templates

When using the pattern templates, trace the pattern onto tracing paper, and transfer all the stitching lines. Adhere the traced patterns with fusible web or spray adhesive to firm cardstock for ease in tracing shapes onto the felt. In many cases, the outline of the pattern template is the outermost stitching line and therefore represents the exact shape of the finished piece. Because you won't need seam allowances for turning seams, the felt pieces are cut out about ⅛″ beyond the stitching lines; so leave at least ¼″ between pieces as you trace. Trace the pattern templates directly onto the right side of the felt using an air- or water-soluble fabric marker for light colors or a chalk marker for dark colors.

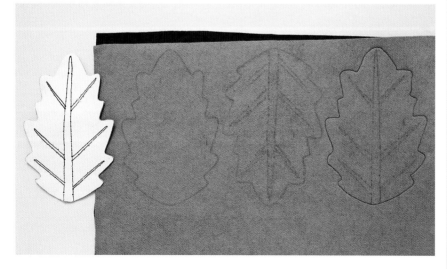

Trace around pattern templates.

Transferring Detail Lines

To transfer detail and top-stitching lines from the pattern template to the fabric, use a large embroidery needle or a stylus to punch holes in the templates along the topstitching lines. Then use an air- or water-soluble fabric marker to mark the dots on the fabric and connect them to form the lines.

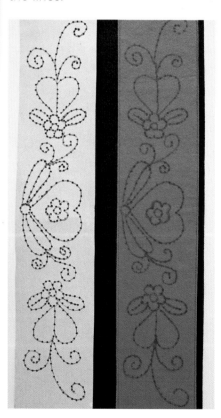

Transfer detail and topstitching lines.

Stitching, then Cutting

Many of the projects call for stitching along the outlines and marked topstitching lines, and THEN cutting just outside the stitched lines. You'll find that this method simplifies the stitching process and shortens your cutting time. It's much easier to move the fabric under the sewing machine needle or the felting machine if you can do it before cutting out the individual pieces. **So be sure to pay attention to the sequence in the instructions, and cut out the pieces only when instructed.**

Needle Felting

At its most basic, needle felting is simply joining fibers to fabric by repeatedly piercing the fabric surface with a felting needle. This process caries fibers through the surface and permanently entangles them with the fabric. You can needle felt with a single needle, a multineedle tool, or a felting machine, but the process is all the same.

Needle Felting by Hand

When needle felting by hand, place the fabric on a foam felting pad or felting brush, place the fibers on top of the fabric, and pierce the surface of the fabric with the felting needle. You only have to pierce the surface to attach the fibers to the felt. If you pierce too deeply, you will carry the fibers deeply into the foam pad, and the back side of your work will be fuzzy.

Needle Felting by Machine

To make quick work of needle felting, you can use a machine such as the Baby Lock Embellisher, which is specifically designed for this function. Although the Embellisher looks like a sewing machine, it consists simply of a multineedle holder attached to an arm that moves up and down rapidly, joining fibers or layers of fabric together by entangling them mechanically. There are no feed dogs, so you move the fabric around under the needles as they go up and down. You will quickly learn to coordinate the needle speed and fabric movement—the process is much like free-motion stitching.

The Embellisher can accommodate up to seven needles, and they can be removed individually for detail work or needle replacement. The most important tip to remember is **always** end with the needles in the uppermost position, completely out of the fabric, to avoid breaking the needles.

Needle-felted surface embellishment

Mosaic Appliqué Needle Felting

You can needle felt two layers of felt together to create a single piece of fabric with your own design permanently embedded in the fibers. This technique is called mosaic felting.

The fibers will meld together just as when you use roving, but mosaic felting has a much crisper edge and contemporary look to it. This technique is showcased in several of the A Place for Everything projects (pages 32–46), in which a sheet of mosaic appliqué fabric is cut into shapes and applied to the surface of the project.

Mosaic appliqué needle felting

Needle Felting with Yarn

You can needle felt with plain or novelty yarns to create outlines, add an allover texture, or accentuate a shape or a form. To get started, begin at one end of the yarn, and hold the yarn taut with your free hand while piercing the yarn and the felt surface with the felting needle. This method works well with either a single needle or a felting machine.

Needle felting with yarn

Needle Felting onto Sheer Fabric

You can create an interesting textural contrast by needle felting wool, wool fibers, silk fibers, or yarns and trims onto a sheer fabric background such as organza or tulle, as in the Bed of Roses Sheer Bed Scarf (page 73). The action of the felting needle tends to shred the sheer fabric somewhat, so be careful not to get carried away. To avoid problems, you can place an additional layer of felt on the underside of the sheer layer to protect the sheer fabric and provide a firm layer of foundation.

Needle felting on sheer fabric

Shading with Needle Felting

To create the illusion of dimension and light and shade, needle felt colored roving in darker shades first, and then gradually add lighter shades over it in thin layers, blending each layer slightly with the layers beneath to create complex hues and dappled light. The trick here is to contrast the strong light of your highlights with correspondingly strong dark shadows cast in a consistent direction from the imagined light source. For a truly luminous highlight, add a final touch of silk roving to catch the light.

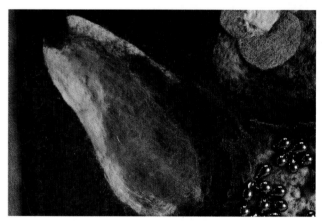

Shading with needle felting

Fulling

Create your own felted wool by washing woven or knitted woolen fabric in a washing machine with hot water and then drying with high heat to felt the fibers together. The process, known as fulling, will generally cause shrinkage, so be sure to allow extra yardage, and wait to cut out the pieces for your project until after you have completed the fulling process.

To full your wool, wash it in hot water with 1/2 cup of baking soda or a mild detergent. Be sure to wash colors separately. Then fluff the fabric dry on high heat, and remove it promptly from the dryer to avoid permanent wrinkles. If you find you have shrunk the fabric more than you intended to, press it lightly with a pressing cloth and a steam iron, stretching the fabric a bit as you press. Fulling will also soften the fabric. Depending on the fiber content, the resulting fulled fabric can vary from nubby to fuzzy. It's fun to experiment and see what you can create.

You can also use this process on wool felt to thicken the fibers and soften the fabric.

Fulled wool

Felt Appliqué

Create beautiful, crisp, clean designs and intricate patterns by simply sewing one piece of felt onto another. I like to embellish my felt appliqué with contrasting top stitching and multiple layers of colorful felt. If you get carried away and your appliqués become too thick to stitch down, use fabric glue to attach them to your background surface. Because you will probably have already done extensive top stitching, only you will know that the pieces aren't stitched on; they'll work just fine, and they'll look spectacular.

Felt appliqué

Reverse, or Subtractive, Felt Appliqué

Reverse felt appliqué is one of my favorite techniques. Patterns and motifs are stitched through layers of fabric, then selected layers of fabric are cut away to reveal the layers below, creating a dimensional and colorful surface. The technique works especially well with felt because the thickness of the felt adds an extra dimension. Furthermore, because felt doesn't fray, you can cut the felt away very close to your top stitching without endangering the integrity of the stitching line to create a stained-glass-style outline that offers many design possibilities.

Reverse, or subtractive, appliqué

Sculpting with Felt

Felt is such a wonderfully versatile fabric. It can be soft and cuddly or crisp and clean-edged, but it is absolutely a stellar choice for creating in three dimensions. With the strategic addition of channels for armature wires, stiff fusible interfacing, or darts and top stitching, there's really no limit to what you can create.

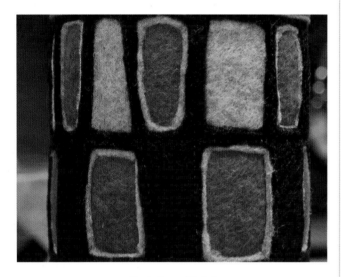

Sculpting with felt

Couching

Instead of needle felting yarn or trim onto your felt project, you might want to couch it on. Set your sewing machine to a wide, long zigzag stitch, and use an open-toe embroidery foot, if available. Position the yarn or trim between the two prongs of the foot, and zigzag over the yarn to attach it to your fabric. You can make the couching thread almost invisible by using thread that matches the yarn or trim, or you can use a contrasting or metallic thread as your couching thread to emphasize the stitches.

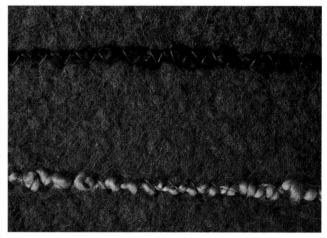

Couching

Dining in Style—
Autumn Leaves Accents

Spice up your dining with these textural table
accessories made in soft fall colors. You can
almost hear the rustle of leaves and feel the
crisp breezes.

Celebrate Mother Nature's boundless beauty with this stylish table runner sprinkled generously with a host of autumn leaf appliqués. A full palette of colors and natural shapes creates an artful design and allover pattern.

falling leaves table runner

Materials

See pages 7–11 for tools and materials.

Note: yardage amounts are based on 36″-wide felt.

- Moss green and barn red wool felt: ½ yard of each color
- Pumpkin wool felt: 1¼ yards
- Honey mustard wool felt: ¼ yard
- Threads to match felt colors
- Sulky KK2000 repositionable adhesive spray
- Fabric marker: chalk, or air- or water-soluble marker

Instructions

See pages 12–16 for working with felt.

1. Use the maple leaf pattern on page 25 and the leaf patterns of your choice on the pattern pullout at the back of the book to make templates (refer to Making and Using Pattern Templates on page 12). Transfer all the markings to the templates.

2. Cut 1 moss green felt rectangle 18″ × 36″ for the runner top. Cut 2 pumpkin felt rectangles 18″ × 36″. One piece will be used as the liner for the runner to add thickness, and the other will be used for the back of the runner.

3. From the barn red felt, cut 4 strips 1″ × 18″ and 4 strips 1″ × 36″ for the borders.

Align the 1″ × 18″ red strips along the short edges of the green rectangle, and zigzag stitch over the edges to create the side borders. Align the 1″ × 36″ red strips along the long edges of the unit, overlapping the red strips at the corners, and stitch. Repeat this process to add borders to 1 pumpkin rectangle.

4. Stack the moss green and pumpkin layers, placing the extra pumpkin rectangle between them. Use repositionable adhesive to hold the layers in place. Topstitch all the way around the outside of the runner, close to the outer edge of the border. Topstitch again close to the inside edge of the border.

Topstitch around edges of border.

5. Trace and cut out 16 leaves using the remaining felt. Transfer all the markings to the felt.

Trace and cut out leaves; transfer markings.

6. Scatter the leaves randomly over the runner. Use repositionable adhesive to hold them in place. Topstitch along the outlines of the leaves and the vein patterns using free-motion or straight stitching as preferred.

Topstitch leaves and veins

FINISHED PLACEMAT SIZE: 13½˝ × 18˝

Make these generously sized placemats to coordinate with the Falling Leaves Table Runner (page 18) or as stand-alone accents for your fall table. The measurements and yardage given are for a pair of matching placemats. If you prefer, you can change the color combinations for each place setting.

falling leaves placemats

Materials

See pages 7–11 for tools and materials.

Note: yardage amounts are based on 36˝-wide felt.

For 2 placemats:

- Moss green wool felt: ½ yard
- Pumpkin wool felt: ⅔ yard
- Barn red wool felt: ½ yard
- Honey mustard wool felt: ¼ yard
- Heavyweight fast2fuse: 2 pieces 13½˝ × 18˝
- Threads to match felt colors
- Sulky KK2000 repositionable adhesive spray
- Fabric marker: chalk, or air- or water-soluble marker

Instructions

See pages 12–16 for working with felt.

1. Use 3 leaf patterns of your choice on the pattern pullout at the back of the book to make templates (refer to Making and Using Pattern Templates on page 12). Transfer all the markings to the templates.

2. Cut the moss green felt into 2 rectangles 13½˝ × 18˝. Cut the pumpkin felt into 2 rectangles 13½˝ × 18˝.

3. From the barn red felt, cut 8 strips 1˝ × 13½˝ and 8 strips 1˝ × 18˝ for the borders.

For each placemat, align the 1˝ × 13½˝ red strips along the short edges of a moss green felt rectangle, and zigzag stitch over the edges to create the side borders. Align the 1˝ × 18˝ red strips along the long edges of the unit, overlapping the red strips at the corners, and stitch. Repeat with the pumpkin rectangles.

4. For each placemat, stack together the moss green and pumpkin layers, placing the fast2fuse between them. Fuse the layers together. Topstitch all the way around the outside, close to the outer edge of the border. Topstitch again close to the inside edge of the border.

Topstitch around edges of border.

5. Trace and cut out 3 leaves for each placemat from the remaining felt. Transfer all the markings to the felt.

6. Arrange the leaves in one corner of each placemat. Use repositionable adhesive to hold them in place. Topstitch along the outlines of the leaves and vein patterns using free-motion or straight stitching as preferred.

Topstitch leaves and veins.

FINISHED COASTER SIZE: 4½″ × 4½″

Accentuate the earthy palette of your autumn décor with these distinctive felt coasters featuring reverse appliqué oak leaves. Simple to make and perfect for every fall table, a stack of these tied up with raffia would make the perfect hostess gift to show your appreciation for an autumn celebration.

leaves of gold coasters

Materials

See pages 7–11 for tools and materials.

- Moss green, pumpkin, and barn red wool felt: 1 square 5″ × 5″ of each color for each coaster

- Threads to match felt colors

- Fabric marker: chalk, or air- or water-soluble marker

Instructions

See pages 12–16 for working with felt.

1. Use the coaster and oak leaf pattern on page 23 to make templates (refer to Making and Using Pattern Templates on page 12). Transfer all the markings to the templates.

2. For each coaster, stack the felt squares with the barn red on top, alternating the moss green and pumpkin squares in the middle. Trace the coaster template onto the red layer of each stack. Stitch around the coaster outline.

3. Arrange the leaf template diagonally inside the stitched coaster outlines, and trace the leaf. Transfer the markings for the veins.

Trace leaf template; transfer markings.

4. Topstitch along the outlines of the leaves and the vein patterns.

Topstitch leaves and veins.

5. Trim the outside of the coasters close to the stitching lines.

6. Use small sharp-pointed scissors to cut away the barn red layer of felt inside the leaves, carefully cutting close to the topstitched outlines and veins—be careful not to cut through the other layers.

Cut away red felt layer inside leaves and close to outlines and veins.

Coaster and oak leaf pattern

FINISHED NAPKIN RING SIZE: 4˝ × 5˝

FINISHED VOTIVE COVER SIZE: 4˝ × 5˝

Add fall color, rich texture, and seasonal style to your table with these needle-felted maple leaf accents. Choose a palette of sumptuous wool roving in tawny autumn shades to create the look of sun-dappled maple leaves. The same design works equally well as a napkin ring or as a slip-on cover for a votive holder.

felted leaves napkin rings and votive covers

Materials

See pages 7–11 for tools and materials.

- Barn red wool felt: 1 piece 6˝ × 9˝ for each napkin ring or votive cover
- Gold, orange, green, yellow, red, and brown wool roving: small wisps of each color
- Threads to match felt colors
- Fabric marker: chalk, or air- or water-soluble marker
- Felting needle and pad, or needle-felting machine

Instructions

See pages 12–16 for working with felt.

1. Arrange wisps of the roving in a random pattern on the barn red felt pieces. Needle felt the roving thoroughly to create an allover pattern, melding the roving with the background fabric.

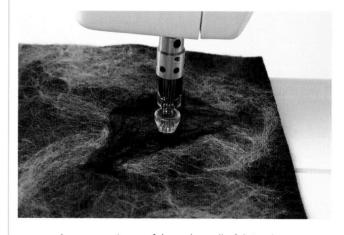

Arrange roving on felt, and needle felt in place.

2. Use the maple leaf pattern below to make a template (refer to Making and Using Pattern Templates on page 12). Transfer the vein markings to the template.

3. Trace the template onto the wrong side of the needle-felted fabric twice for each ring or votive cover. Topstitch along the vein patterns. Cut out the leaves along the outlines.

Topstitch veins, and cut out leaves.

4. Layer pairs of leaves with edges even and needle-felted patterns facing out. Needle felt the leaves together at the outermost edges of the sides, leaving the centers open.

Needle felt leaves together at outer edges.

5. Insert a votive candle holder or napkin between the leaves.

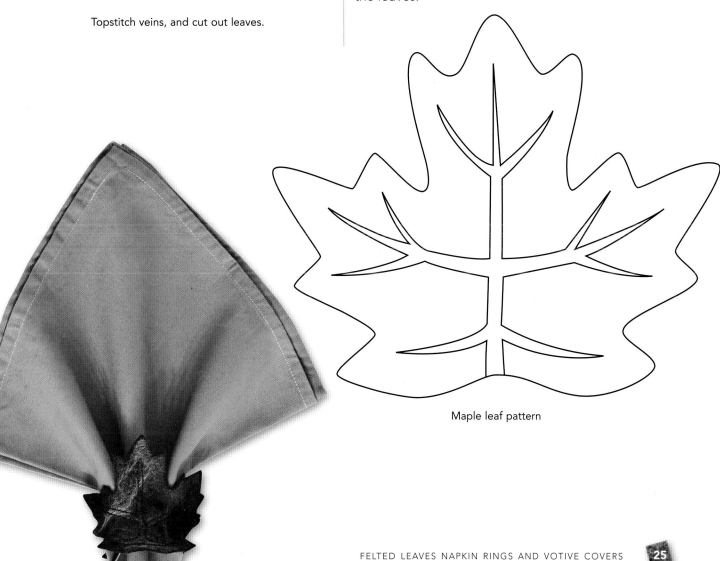

Maple leaf pattern

FINISHED LEAF SIZE: 5″ × 7½″

What better way to celebrate the glory of Mother Nature's autumn extravaganza than with a bouquet of beautifully sculpted oak leaves over your fall dining table. The secret to these fool-the-eye leaves is in the top stitching that gives dimension and form to each leaf. These will surely become an important autumn highlight of your seasonal décor.

stems and leaves centerpiece

Materials

See pages 7–11 for tools and materials.

Note: yardage amount is based on 36″-wide felt. Materials listed will make 24 double-layer leaves.

- Copper, yellow, barn red, teddy bear brown, pumpkin spice, and mustard yellow wool felt for leaves: 2 pieces 18″ × 12″ of each color

- Moss green wool felt: ⅓ yard

- Threads to match felt colors

- Simply Stems, ¼″ diameter, assorted lengths: 1 package (9 pieces)

- 22-gauge wrapped florist wire: 24 pieces, each 8″ long

- Fabric glue

- Fabric marker: chalk, or air- or water-soluble marker

Instructions

See pages 12–16 for working with felt.

1. Use the Stems and Leaves oak leaf pattern on the pattern pullout at the back of the book to make a template (refer to Making and Using Pattern Templates on page 12). Transfer all the markings to the template.

2. Layer pairs of coordinating colors of felt, and trace the leaf template 24 times. Transfer all the markings to the felt. Topstitch around the outlines of all the traced leaves, and cut out the leaves close to the stitching.

Trace, stitch, and cut out leaves.

3. Fold each leaf in half lengthwise. Match the marked center lines, and stitch a channel for the florist wire from the tip to the bottom of each leaf.

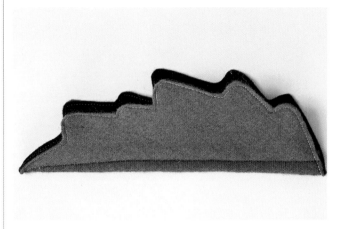

Fold leaves, and stitch center channels.

4. Fold each leaf at each set of marked vein lines, matching the lines. Stitch the veins from the outer edge of each leaf to the center channel stitching. Stitch close to the folds, and secure the stitching at the beginning and end of each row of stitches by backtacking.

Fold leaves, and stitch veins.

5. Insert florist wire into the center channel of each leaf. The wire should extend at least 1½″ beyond the end of the leaf.

Insert florist wire into channels.

6. To make the stem covers from moss green felt, cut 3 strips 1¼″ × 16″, 3 strips 1¼″ × 25″, and 3 strips 1¼″ × 31″. Fold each strip in half lengthwise, and stitch close to the cut edges.

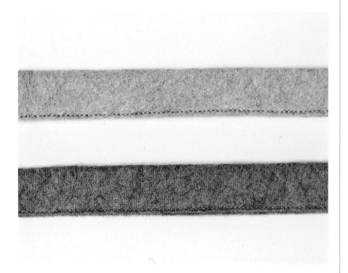

Fold and stitch stem covers.

7. Insert a Simply Stem into each stem cover, trimming the stem cover to fit as needed. Insert the florist wires of 2 or 3 leaves of assorted colors into one end of each stem cover until the wires are no longer visible, and glue in place. Glue the opposite ends of the stem covers closed. Arrange the stems in a tall vase with pebbles or marbles, or use the soft vase wrap featured on page 29.

Cover stems, and insert leaves.

Costarring with the stems and leaves as the show-stopping centerpiece of your Autumn Leaves dining table is this unique reverse appliqué soft vase wrap that combines the design elements of contemporary cloisonné with the texture and feel of rustic wool blankets. The upper layers of felt are cut away close to the top-stitched outlines and veins of the stylized leaf motifs to create a bold allover pattern. The vessel can be filled with marbles and used as a stand-alone vase, or you can tuck a cylindrical vase filled with water inside to keep flowers or greenery fresh.

layered felt vase wrap

Materials

See pages 7–11 for tools and materials.

- Barn red wool felt: 1 piece 14″ × 16″, 2 squares 6″ × 6″

- Moss green wool felt: 2 pieces 14″ × 16″

- Pumpkin wool felt: 1 piece 14″ × 16″

- Threads to match felt colors

- Heavyweight fast2fuse: 1 square 6″ × 6″

- Fabric marker: chalk, or air- or water-soluble marker

Instructions

See pages 12–16 for working with felt.

1. Use the vase side and bottom patterns on the pattern pullout at the back of the book to make templates (refer to Making and Using Pattern Templates on page 12). Transfer the leaves and all the other markings.

2. Use the vase bottom template to cut out 2 barn red felt vase bottoms from the 6″ × 6″ squares. Also, cut out a vase bottom from fast2fuse, and trim ¼″ from the outer edges. Center the fast2fuse circle between the 2 felt circles, and follow the manufacturer's instructions to fuse the layers together. Stitch around the outer edges of the circles with a medium-width and medium-length zigzag stitch, positioning the fabric so that when the needle moves to the right, it falls just off the edge of the fabric.

Fuse and stitch layers together.

3. Trace the vase and leaves onto 1 piece of the moss green felt. Cut out along the traced vase outline. Set aside.

Trace vase template onto 1 felt layer. Cut out.

4. Stack the remaining 3 felt pieces with moss green on the bottom, pumpkin in the middle, and barn red on top. Trace the vase onto the red felt layer. Stitch around the traced outline.

Topstitch vase outline onto stacked felt.

5. With the barn red layer on top, arrange and pin the marked moss green piece on top of the stack, matching the cut edges with the stitched outline. Topstitch over the leaf outlines and veins. Use sharp-pointed scissors to cut away the moss green felt layer close to the stitching around the outside of the leaves.

Stitch leaves, and cut away top layer close to stitching.

6. Cut away the moss green and the barn red layers inside the leaves, being careful to maintain a thin felt outline around the stitching on the veins and outlines.

Cut away 2 layers inside leaves.

7. Cut out the vase close to the stitching. Match the straight edges, and fold the vase with right sides out. Zigzag stitch the seam, positioning the fabric so that when the needle moves to the right, it falls just off the edge of the fabric.

Stitch side seam of vase.

8. Pin the vase and the vase bottom together, matching edges. Zigzag stitch around the bottom of the vase through all layers, positioning the fabric so that when the needle moves to the right, it falls just off the edge of the fabric. Zigzag around the top to finish the top edge of the vase.

Stitch bottom to sides.

Zigzag stitch around top of vase.

A Place for Everything—
Organizing Accents

Stake your claim as you transform an ordinary corner into your own personalized craft nook, writer's lair, or home office. These small but colorful coordinated accessories work together to help you create order out of chaos and to showcase your personal style.

FINISHED DESKTOP CADDY SIZE:
27″ × 2¾″

This contemporary desktop caddy, inspired by a votive candle holder, is just the thing to corral all those little things that tend to clutter your desk: stamps, coins, paperclips, erasers, thumbtacks, and so on. Needle-felted mosaic squares lend clean lines and colorful style to this clever office accent.

desktop caddy

Materials

See pages 7–11 for tools and materials.

- Honey mustard wool felt: 2 pieces 2¾″ × 27¼″
- Cardinal red wool felt: 1 piece 4″ × 9″
- Moss green wool felt: scrap strips 4″ long × random widths
- Honey mustard wool felt: scrap strips 4″ long × random widths ranging from ¼″ to 1″
- Copper wool felt: scrap strips 4″ long × random widths
- Threads to match felt colors
- Glass votive holders: 7
- Fabric marker: chalk, or air- or water-soluble marker
- Felting needle and pad, or needle-felting machine

Instructions

See pages 12–16 for working with felt.

1. Use the desktop caddy pattern template on page 34 to make a template (refer to Making and Using Pattern Templates on page 12).

2. Place the template on a honey mustard felt strip with the top and bottom edges of the template aligned with the top and bottom edges of the felt, and the left top edge of the template ¼″ in from one short end of the felt strip. Mark the sides of the template. Move the template over, leaving ⅜″ between marks at the upper edge of the felt strip, and trace the template again. Repeat to trace the template 7 times total. You should have a ¼″ seam allowance left at the other end of the felt strip. Repeat with the other honey mustard strip.

Trace template 7 times to mark stitching lines.

3. Arrange several random-width strips of copper, moss green, and honey mustard felt on the cardinal red felt to create a striped pattern. Needle felt the strips solidly in place to permanently join them. Trim away the uneven outer edges, cut into 1″-wide strips, then cut the needle-felted mosaic into 14 squares 1″ × 1″.

Create needle-felted mosaic felt. Cut into 14 squares.

4. Arrange and pin the squares diagonally on the marked honey mustard felt strips, centering the squares between the marked lines. Stitch from the top to the bottom of each square to secure.

Stitch squares onto felt strips.

5. Arrange the 2 embellished strips with the wrong sides together. Match the marked lines at the top and the bottom, and pin the strips together at each interval.

6. Stitch along each marked line from top to bottom, and across the top and bottom edges. Use a securing stitch at both ends.

7. Trim the seam allowance evenly at each end of the joined felt strips.

8. Insert the 7 votive holders between the felt strips.

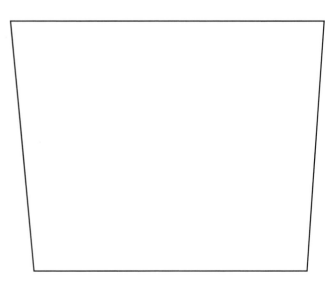

Stitch felt strips together, and insert votives.

Desktop caddy pattern

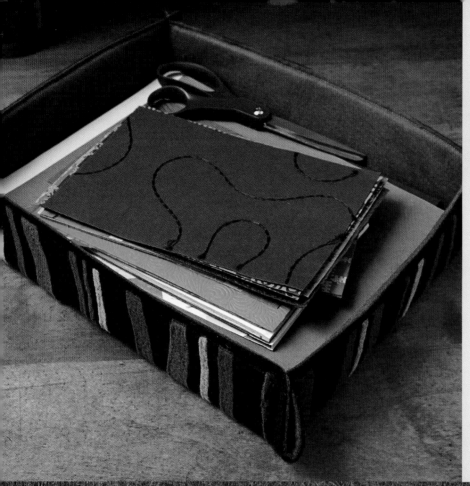

FINISHED PAPER TRAY SIZE:
9″ × 12″ × 2½″

This updated twist on a traditional soft-fabric tray lends style and flair to your home office. Rich earth-toned felt stripes are needle felted onto a solid felt background for a crisp contemporary mosaic look.

mosaic stripes needle-felted paper tray

Materials

See pages 7–11 for tools and materials.

- Cardinal red wool felt: 1 piece 12″ × 14″, 1 piece 17″ × 20″

- Moss green wool felt: 1 piece 17″ × 20″, scrap strips 12″ long × random widths

- Honey mustard wool felt: scrap strips: 12″ long × random widths ranging from ¼″ to 1″

- Copper wool felt: scrap strips: 12″ long × random widths

- Threads to match moss green and cardinal red felt

- Heavyweight fast2fuse: 2 pieces 2⅛″ × 11¾″, 2 pieces 2⅛″ × 9¼″, 1 piece 9″ × 12″

- Sulky KK2000 repositionable adhesive spray

- Chalk fabric marker

- Felting needle and pad, or needle-felting machine

Instructions

See pages 12–16 for working with felt.

1. Arrange several random-width scrap strips of copper, moss green, and honey mustard felt on the 12″ × 14″ piece of cardinal red felt to create a striped pattern. Needle felt the strips solidly in place to permanently join them.

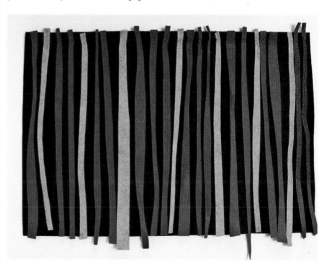

Needle felt strips onto panel.

2. Trim away the uneven outer edges of the felted mosaic. Measure and cut perpendicular to the stripes 2 pieces 2½″ × 12″ for the long sides of the tray and 2 pieces 2½″ × 9½″ for the short sides.

3. Referring to the Paper Tray Diagram on page 37, use a chalk marker to draw the outline of the tray and all markings on the 17″ × 20″ piece of cardinal red felt.

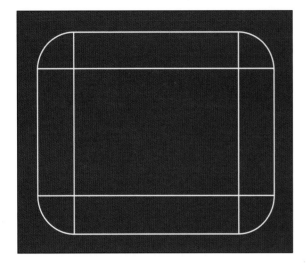

Measure and mark outline and details of tray.

4. Spray repositionable adhesive on the wrong side of the striped side strips. Position the strips along the sides of the tray as indicated. Press lightly with your fingers to adhere the strips to the background fabric. Stitch around each strip close to the cut edges.

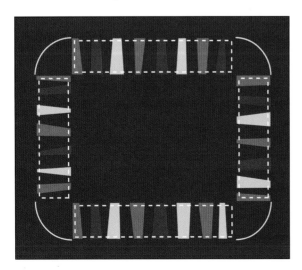

Stitch around strips close to edges.

5. Arrange the stitched cardinal red layer on top of the 17″ × 20″ piece of moss green felt. Match the edges, and pin the layers together. Stitch around 3 sides of the tray bottom and the corresponding 3 outer edges of the tray sides, leaving the corners open. Insert the fast2fuse pieces for three sides and the bottom between the layers, sliding the pieces into the stitched channels.

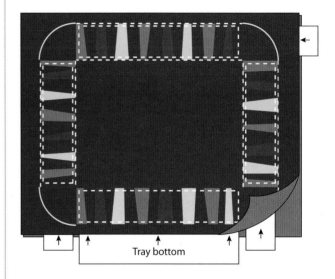

Tray bottom

Insert fast2fuse between layers.

6. Stitch around the remaining unstitched side of the tray bottom and unstitched outer edge, leaving the corners open. Slide the remaining strip of fast2fuse into the remaining side channel.

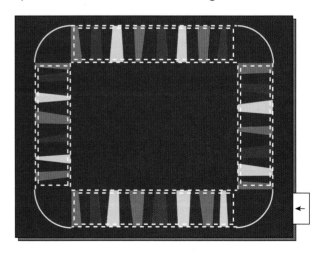

Stitch last channel.

7. Stitch the corners of the channels and around the curved markings on all 4 corners of the tray. Trim away the excess felt close to the stitching.

Stitch corners to enclose fast2fuse.

8. Topstitch the tray bottom to create an allover pattern and to stabilize the tray base. Press to fuse the layers together.

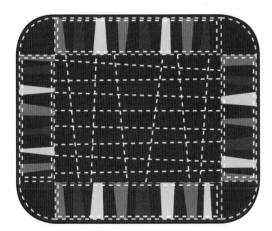

Stitch pattern on tray bottom.

9. Match the corners, and pinch the felt together to form a pleat toward the outside at each corner. Stitch across each pleat to form the sides of the tray.

Stitch across pleat at each corner to make tray sides.

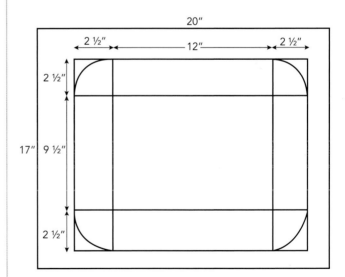

Paper tray cutting and sewing diagram

FINISHED PENCIL CUP SIZE:
5¼″ × 2½″ DIAMETER

Lend artful style to your home office by transforming a tea canister into an eye-catching pencil cup. This project showcases a multilayered reverse appliqué technique that creates a colorful and textural accent for your desk.

sculpted felt pencil cup

Materials

See pages 7–11 for tools and materials.

- Cardinal red, yellow, and dark orange wool felt: 1 piece 7″ × 9½″ * of each color

- Threads to match felt colors

- Tea canister: 5¼″ × 2½″ diameter*, labels removed (I used a Republic of Tea canister.)

- Fabric marker: chalk, or air- or water-soluble marker

*Adjust dimensions as needed to fit your tea canister.

Instructions

See pages 12–16 for working with felt.

1. Layer the 3 pieces of felt with dark orange on the top, yellow in the middle, and cardinal red on bottom. Measure and mark a 5″ × 9″ rectangle centered on the layered pieces. Stitch around the marked outline.

2. Measure and mark 3 evenly divided horizontal sections on the rectangle. Mark a somewhat random windowpane pattern of slightly slanted lines from top to bottom. Stitch over all the marked lines within the 5″ × 9″ rectangle in a continuous pattern.

Measure, mark, and stitch pattern onto layered felt.

3. Along the short side edges of the rectangle, cut away all 3 layers of the felt close to the outline stitching.

4. Along the top and bottom edges of the rectangle, cut away the cardinal red and yellow layers close to the outline stitching. Fold the remaining dark orange layer over the top and bottom edges of the patterned rectangle to form bands, and topstitch the bands in place.

Trim away side edges, and fold to form bands on top and bottom.

5. To create the sculpted surface, use sharp-pointed scissors to cut away 1 layer to expose the yellow felt or cut away 2 layers to expose the dark orange felt. Cut close to, but not into, the stitching. Leave some sections of the cardinal red felt intact to create a pattern with 3 different colors and 3 layers of texture.

Cut away felt layers to create pattern.

6. Pinch together the side edges with wrong sides together, and hand stitch.

Hand stitch sides together.

7. Slide the cover onto the tea canister.

FINISHED BOX SIZE: 10″ × 13″ × 5″

Dramatic shading, silken sheen, and bead-encrusted detail lend this decorative storage box the upscale and opulent look of a sculpted bas-relief work of art. Look closely, and you'll see that the pears, pomegranates, and persimmons still life is actually created from needle-felted appliqués and needle-felted shading. that work together to fool the eye. The generously sized box provides an attractive place to stow projects-in-progress to keep clutter to a minimum.

felted fruits decorative box

Materials

See pages 7–11 for tools and materials.

- Purchased fabric- or suede-covered box approximately 10″ × 13″ × 5″

- Brown and mellow yellow wool felt: 1 piece 9″ × 12″ of each color

- Burnt orange wool felt: 1 piece 4″ × 12″

- Moss green wool felt: 1 piece 2″ × 6″

- Deep red felted woven wool or wool felt: 1 piece 5″ × 9″

- Wool roving: red orange, yellow, brown, and ivory

- Thick deep cranberry felted wool novelty yarn

- Silk hankies in coordinating palette

- Novelty pomegranate seed glass beads: 60, approximately ¼″ long

- Fabric glue

- Fabric marker: chalk, or air- or water-soluble marker

- Felting needle and pad, or needle-felting machine

Instructions

See pages 12–16 for working with felt.

1. Use the fruit patterns on the pattern pullout at the back of the book to make templates (refer to Making and Using Pattern Templates on page 12). Transfer all the markings to the templates.

2. Trace and cut out 1 large and 2 medium pears from mellow yellow felt, 3 persimmons from burnt orange felt, 3 persimmon tops from moss green felt, and 2 pomegranates from deep red felted woven wool or felt.

Trace and cut out fruits.

3. Use the placement guide on the pattern pullout at the back of the book to arrange the fruit pieces on the brown felt, and needle felt them onto the background.

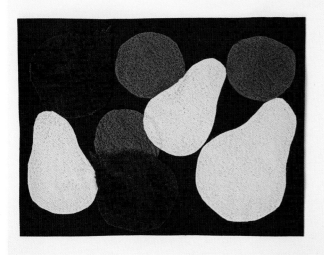

Needle felt fruits onto background.

4. Blend small bits of fiber from the silk hankies with the wool roving to add shading, highlights, stems, and blemishes to the fruit.

5. To make the tops of the persimmons, arrange a moss green felt top piece on each persimmon, bringing the short ends of the top piece together to create a dimensional blossom shape. Attach the inner edges of the persimmon tops to the surface of the persimmon by needle felting with yellow roving. Leave the outer edges free.

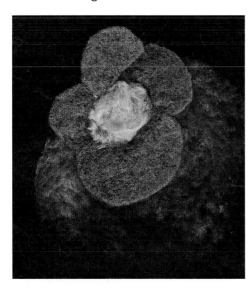

Needle felt persimmon tops in place.

6. To create the inside of the beaded pomegranate, needle felt ivory roving onto the pomegranate, leaving the outer edges of red showing. Hand stitch the pomegranate seed beads individually to create several clusters inside the fruit. Hand stitch a few single seed beads to the background as shown in the photo on page 40.

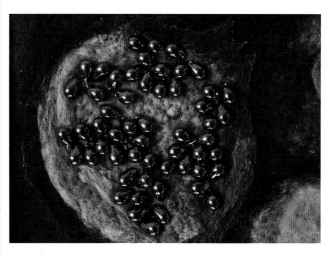

Needle felt roving, and hand stitch beads onto pomegranate.

7. Center the embellished panel on the box lid, and mark the placement. Remove the panel, and apply fabric glue inside the marked area. Carefully place the panel onto the glue, and press with fingertips to attach permanently.

8. Measure, cut, and glue the felted yarn around the outer edges of the panel.

Glue yarn around panel.

FINISHED FRAME SIZE: 8˝ × 10˝

This project showcases an easy way to transform an ordinary inexpensive clear plastic sleeve–type frame into an extraordinary accent piece for your home office. The needle-felted sleeve simply slides right over the frame. This frame is decorated with dimensional fruit appliqués and a bit of beading to coordinate with the palette and motifs of the home office projects. However, this idea for a sleeve-type cover could be interpreted in any theme or color scheme to work in any room of the house.

felted fruits appliqué picture frame

Materials

See pages 7–11 for tools and materials.

- Clear plastic standing frame: 8˝ × 10˝

- Deep orange wool felt: 2 pieces 9˝ × 12˝

- Cardinal red wool felt: 1 piece 9˝ × 12˝, 1 piece 2˝ × 6˝

- Moss green wool felt: 1 piece 2˝ × 12˝

- Red, orange, yellow cream, pale green, and brown wool roving: small amounts of each color

- Novelty pomegranate glass beads: 7, approximately ¼˝ long:

- Threads to match felt colors

- 4˝ × 6˝ photo

- Permanent fabric adhesive

- Fabric marker: chalk, or air- or water-soluble marker

- Felting needle and pad, or needle-felting machine

Instructions

See pages 12–16 for working with felt.

1. Center the plastic frame on 1 piece of deep orange felt, and trace the outline of the plastic frame onto the felt. Remove the plastic frame. Measure and mark a 4″ × 6″ opening in the center of the traced frame outline.

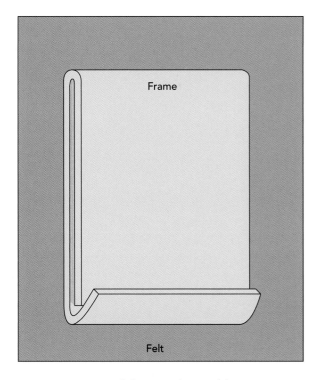

Mark frame outline on felt.

2. Use the patterns on the pattern pullout at the back of the book to make templates for the appliqués (refer to Making and Using Pattern Templates on page 12). Transfer all the markings to the templates.

3. Cut 1 strip ¼″ × 12″ from the moss green felt for the vine. Use the leaf template to cut 10 leaves from the green felt.

4. Trace the appliqué pattern onto the picture frame front, and needle felt a thin strip of moss green felt along the vine on the frame. Arrange the green felt leaves on the vine, and needle felt them in place.

Needle felt vine and leaves onto frame front.

5. Pin the remaining 9″ × 12″ piece of deep orange felt to the wrong side of the needle-felted frame front, matching edges. Stitch around the marked photo opening and across the lower 9″ edge.

Stitch around photo opening and across lower frame edge.

6. Carefully cut out the photo opening close to the stitching. Pin the 9″ × 12″ piece of cardinal red felt to the back of the frame front. Stitch around the sides and top, stitching close to the edge and leaving the lower edge open so that the frame sleeve can slide over the frame.

Cut away picture opening; join front and back.

7. Trace the pear, pomegranate, and persimmon outlines onto the 2″ × 6″ piece of cardinal red felt. Referring to the photo, needle felt the shading and details onto each shape with wool roving. Cut out the fruit pieces along traced outlines.

Needle felt shading and details onto fruit, and cut out.

8. Glue the appliqués in place on the front of the frame, and hand stitch the beads in place.

Glue appliqués, and hand stitch beads onto frame.

9. Glue or tape the photo to the center of an 8″ × 10″ piece of plain paper, and slide it into the plastic photo frame.

10. Slide the felt frame cover over the plastic frame, and adjust as necessary to align with the photo.

Position photo on paper, and slide into frame.

FINISHED BOOKSHELF TRIM SIZE:
3″ WIDE × LENGTH OF SHELF

Here's a great way to transform an ordinary laminate wood bookshelf into an attractive and color-coordinated focal point of your home office décor. The beaded and scalloped shelf borders are created with a special cutting guide that allows you to make uniform scallops quickly and easily. You can layer the scallops, add a strip of needle-felted mosaic edging, and embellish with a few glass beads to create a customized artist's bookcase that's anything but ordinary.

needle-felted bookshelf trim

Materials

See pages 7–11 for tools and materials.

- Cardinal red wool felt: 1 piece 6″ × 18″, 1 piece 3″ × length of shelf + 2″ for each shelf

- Moss green wool felt: 1 piece 3″ x length of shelf + 2″, scrap strips 6″ long x random widths from ½″ to 1½″

- Honey mustard and copper wool felt: scrap strips 6″ long × random widths from ½″ to 1½″ of each color

- Novelty pomegranate glass beads in size of choice

- Threads to match felt colors

- Sulky KK2000 repositionable adhesive spray

- Double-sided tape or hook-and-loop tape

- Fabric marker: chalk, or air- or water-soluble marker

- Felting needle and pad, or needle-felting machine

- Fancy Fleece Ruler (optional)

Instructions

See pages 12–16 for working with felt.

1. Spray repositionable adhesive onto the 3″-wide cardinal red strip, and layer the 3″-wide green strip on top of the red strip. Use the scallop pattern on the pattern pullout at the back of the book to make a template (refer to Making and Using Pattern Templates on page 12), or use the Fancy Fleece Ruler. Align the template or scallop ruler so the deepest part of the scallop is 1½″ from the lower edge of the strips. Trace and cut the scallops.

Trace and cut scallops.

2. Use the red layer with outward scallops and the green layer with inward scallops. With straight edges aligned, layer the cut strips with the red layer on top and the points from the green layer centered between the red scallops. Zigzag stitch along the top edge. Pin the layers together, and topstitch around the edge of the red scallops. Hint: You can make trim for 2 shelves from 1 strip if you alternate the colors: red on green and green on red.

Stack and stitch together scalloped layers.

3. Arrange 6″-long strips of copper, moss green, and honey mustard felt on the 6″ × 18″ piece of cardinal red felt to create a striped pattern. Needle felt the stripes solidly onto the red felt to permanently join them. Cut the piece into ½″-wide strips perpendicular to the stripes.

Needle felt stripes onto panel, and cut panel into ½″-wide strips.

4. Position the needle-felted strips end-to-end along the upper edge of the scalloped strip, and stitch the strips in place along both edges. Hand stitch beads to the moss green points.

Attach needle-felted strips, and stitch on beads.

5. Attach the border trim to your bookshelf edges with double-sided adhesive tape or hook-and-loop tape.

Jewel Tones—
Contemporary Folk-Art Accents

Hearts, flowers, and bright paisley swirls combine to create an updated contemporary folk-art style for each of these light-hearted accents. Timeless icons take on new energy when punched up with color, texture, and dimensional embellishments.

FINISHED MEMENTO BOARD SIZE: 20″ × 30″

Hearts and flowers and swirls, oh my! This personalized memento board features eye-catching needle-felted motifs, yarn doodles, and dimensional felt flower embellishments with room for a name or monogram. A grosgrain ribbon grid keeps favorite photos and mementos tucked neatly on display.

memento board

Materials

See pages 7–11 for tools and materials.

- Purple wool felt: 1 piece 26″ × 36″, 2 pieces 6½″ × 26″, 1 square 4″ × 4″

- Peacock wool felt: 2 pieces 4″ × 20″

- Green wool felt: 1 piece 9″ × 12″

- Red wool felt: assorted scraps for letters

- Variegated or brightly colored yarn scraps

- Yellow and red wool roving: small amounts of each color

- ¼″-diameter buttons: 6

- ⅜″-wide purple grosgrain ribbon: 10 yards

- Precut felt flower embellishments: 2 each of purple, green, and pink

- Threads to match felt colors

- Foamcore board: 20″ × 30″

- ¼″ SuperTape double-sided adhesive tape

- Spray adhesive

- Permanent fabric adhesive

- Chalk fabric marker

- Hand-felting needle and pad, or needle-felting machine

Instructions

See pages 12–16 for working with felt.

1. Mark a 3″ border around the 26″ × 36″ piece of purple felt for the board placement. Apply spray adhesive to the back of the foamcore board, and glue the board down smoothly onto the marked area of the felt.

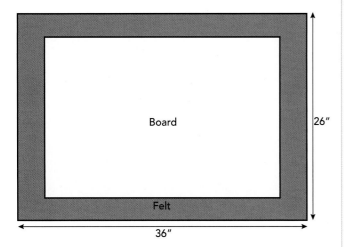

Center and glue board onto felt.

2. Working from the center of each side, apply adhesive and fold the excess felt to the back of the board. To create flat corners, pinch the felt together into a diagonal pleat, and cut away most of the excess felt, leaving a flat flap to glue down smoothly over each corner.

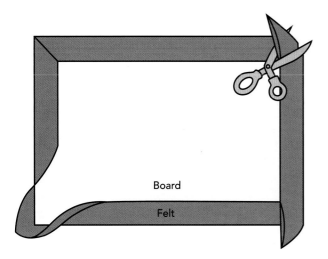

Fold felt to back side, and glue sides and corners.

3. Use a chalk marker to mark horizontal lines 5″ from the top and bottom edges on the front of the board. Mark a horizontal line 2″ from each of those lines. Measure and mark a vertical line 2″ from each side edge; then measure and mark another line 2″ in from the previous line. Measure and mark the centers of the 4 outermost horizontal and vertical lines, and draw diagonal chalk lines to connect the center points, continuing the lines to the edges of the board.

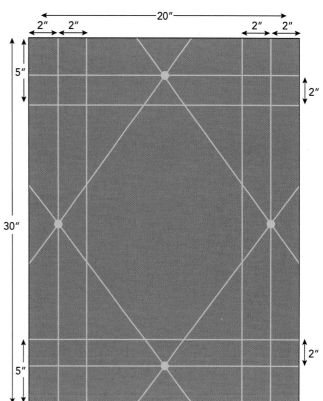

Measure and mark ribbon placement lines.

4. Press the ribbon flat. Cut each piece of ribbon 6″ longer than the chalk line it will cover, to allow for wrapping the ribbon to the back of the board. Apply 3¼″ lengths of SuperTape to the ends of each ribbon. Attach the ribbons over the marked lines, and pull them taut so the SuperTape extends about ¼″ on the front of the board and wraps around to the back side 3″ on each end of the ribbon. Place a small piece of SuperTape between the ribbons at the points where they intersect.

Attach ribbons to board in grid pattern.

Use the decorative panel patterns on the pattern pullout at the back of the book to make templates (refer to Making and Using Pattern Templates on page 12). Transfer all the markings to the templates. Transfer the designs onto the peacock felt strips. Cut out the center heart from purple felt, the side hearts from red felt, and the leaves from green felt. Needle felt the heart, leaves, and swirls onto the peacock strips using roving and yarn. To personalize your project, cut out red felt letters that spell out a name or monogram, and needle felt the letters onto the center of one panel. Hint: Choose a plain font on your computer, and print out the letters to use as patterns.

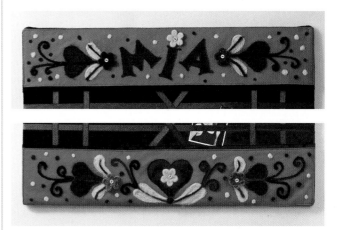

Needle felt designs onto peacock strips.

5. Attach the precut flower embellishments by hand stitching the buttons and flowers where indicated on the pattern. Finish the panels by needle felting red and yellow roving dots randomly over the surface of the panels.

Stitch felt flowers and buttons; needle felt dots.

6. Center the personalized panel ¼″ from the lower edge of one 6½″ × 26″ purple band. Stitch around the edges of the peacock panel. Center the other decorative panel ¼″ from the upper edge of the remaining purple band. Stitch around the edges of the peacock panel.

Stitch panels on purple bands.

7. To attach the upper and lower bands to the board, pin them in place with the peacock panel edges even with the board edges, and fold the excess felt to the back side of the board. Glue the bands in place using permanent fabric adhesive, and cut away the corners as in Step 2.

Hint: Leave the bottom band unattached at its top edge so that it can be used as a pocket to hold light items if desired.

Wrap excess felt on bands to back, and glue in place.

FINISHED PILLOW SIZE: 21″ × 21″

Vibrant colors and whimsical design are the winning combination in this easy-to-make oversized pillow. Soft washed felt and bouclé yarn embellishments add texture and style. Easy assembly and guaranteed success make this a perfect first project for your budding decorator.

four hearts pillow

Materials

See pages 7–11 for tools and materials.

- Washed and felted purple wool felt (refer to Fulling on page 14): 1 square 21″ × 21″, 1 piece 9″ × 21″, 1 piece 13″ × 21″

- Washed and felted red wool felt: 1 piece 9″ × 36″

- Turquoise bouclé yarn: 4 yards

- Threads to match felt and yarn colors

- 1″-wide hook-and-loop tape: 18½″

- 18″ × 18″ pillow form

- Rotary cutter with pinking blade

- Fabric marker: chalk, or air- or water-soluble marker

- Open-toe embroidery foot (optional)

Instructions

See pages 12–16 for working with felt.

1. Use the heart pattern on page 54 to make a template (refer to Making and Using Pattern Templates on page 12). Transfer all the markings to the template.

2. Trace 4 hearts onto the red felt, and transfer all the markings. Use a rotary cutter with a pinking blade to cut out the hearts.

3. Arrange the turquoise bouclé yarn on the marked design on each heart. Beginning at the innermost coil of the design, use a medium zigzag stitch to couch the yarn in place. Secure the yarn and thread ends well by stitching in place several times.

Couch yarn onto heart over marked design.

4. To make the pillow front, measure and mark the 21″ × 21″ purple square to divide it evenly into 4 squares. Pin a heart in each square, spacing them evenly with the points facing the center of the purple square. Stitch around each heart ¼″ from the edge.

Stitch hearts onto pillow front.

5. To make the pillow back, center and pin the loop side of the hook-and-loop tape ¼″ from one long edge of the 9″ × 21″ purple felt piece, and stitch the tape in place. Repeat for the 13″ × 21″ purple felt piece using the hook side of the hook-and-loop tape. Join the hook-and-loop tape strips together to create a 21″ × 21″ square. Treat the pillow back as one piece when assembling the pillow.

Apply hook-and-loop tape, and treat back as one piece.

6. Measure and mark 1″ from the outer edges of the pillow front. Pin together the pillow front and back with right sides out. Stitch along the marked line around all 4 edges to create the pillow cover. Use a rotary cutter with a pinking blade to even up the outside edges of the pillow and create a decorative edge.

7. Open the hook-and-loop tape on the back of the pillow cover, and insert the pillow form.

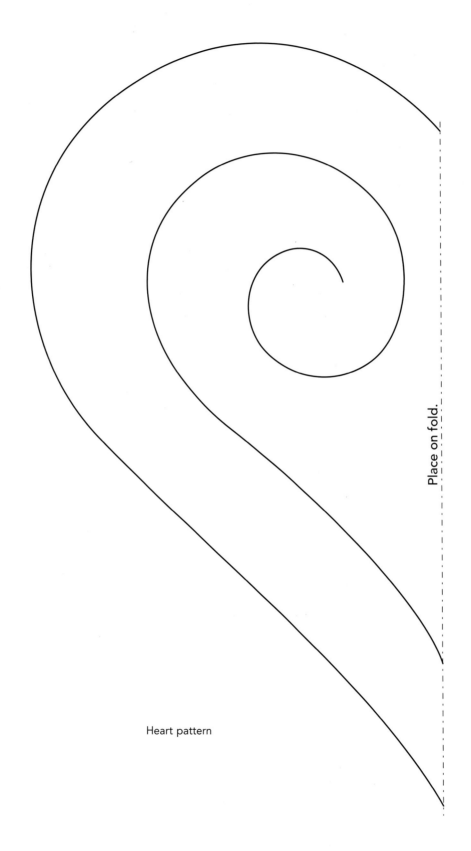

Place on fold.

Heart pattern

Hot colors and cool style define this soft and sassy pillow featuring needle-felted dots, a reverse appliqué paisley heart design, and a felt bead closure for the envelope flap.

paisley envelope pillow

Materials

See pages 7–11 for tools and materials.

- Washed and felted red and turquoise wool felt (refer to Fulling on page 14): 1 piece 24″ × 36″ of each color

- Turquoise and purple wool roving

- Large turquoise felt bead: 1

- Small red felt bead: 1

- Threads to match felt colors

- 16″ × 16″ pillow form

- Rotary cutter with pinking blade

- Fabric marker: chalk, or air- or water-soluble marker

- Felting needle and pad, or needle-felting machine

Instructions

See pages 12–16 for working with felt.

1. Use the flap pattern on the pattern pullout at the back of the book to make a template (refer to Making and Using Pattern Templates on page 12). Transfer all the markings to the template.

2. Cut away the uneven outer edges of the red felt. Measure and mark a 19″ × 19″ square at one end of the felt piece. Align the straight edge of the flap template along one edge of the marked square, and trace the outline of the template to create a continuous piece for the pillow cover back and envelope flap. Use a rotary cutter with a pinking blade to cut the piece out along the marked outline. Transfer the markings from the template to the envelope flap.

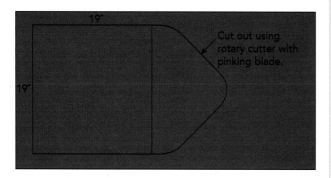

Create pillow cover back and envelope flap.

3. To make the front pillow cover panel, measure and mark a 19″ × 20″ rectangle on the turquoise felt, and cut out the rectangle with the rotary cutter pinking blade. Turn under a 1″ hem on one 19″ edge, and stitch the hem in place close to the cut edge.

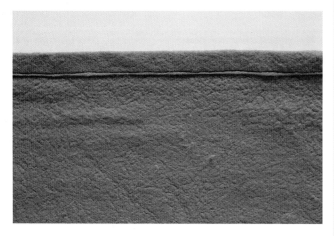

Stitch hem along edge of turquoise rectangle.

4. Trace the outline of the envelope flap template onto the remaining piece of turquoise felt. Cut out the flap with the rotary cutter with the pinking blade. Baste the turquoise flap to the wrong side of the red flap, matching the edges. Stitch the marked paisley heart design through both layers of the envelope flap.

Stitch paisley heart design onto layered flap.

5. Align the hemmed edge of the turquoise front panel with the straight edge of the turquoise flap, and pin the front panel in place, matching all the edges.

Match edges, and pin turquoise front panel onto red back/flap panel.

6. Measure and mark 1˝ from the outer edges of the flap and the layered pillow cover front and back panels. Stitch along the marked lines.

7. To embellish the envelope flap, use the photo as a guide and cut through the red layer close to the heart stitching to create a reverse appliqué design. Cut through both layers in the center of the small teardrop shape near the point of the flap to create a buttonhole. Needle felt random dots of purple and turquoise roving all over the envelope flap for embellishment.

Create reverse appliqué design and needle-felted embellishment on flap.

8. Insert the pillow form into the cover. Smooth the flap over the pillow front, and mark the location for the felt bead button. Remove the pillow form. Stack the small bead onto the large one, and hand stitch the felt beads into place to form a button. Tie off the sewing thread by knotting it securely on the inside of the pillow cover.

FINISHED TOTE SIZE: 8½″ × 11½″

This simple but sassy tote is perfectly designed to keep secret thoughts tucked away in style. Sized to fit a classic composition book, the front flap offers two small pockets for stowing special treasures and a bright dimensional felt flower appliqué to add pizzazz. Easy assembly makes this a perfect project for young sewers.

purs-onal diary tote

Materials

See pages 7–11 for tools and materials.

- Purple wool felt: 1 piece 10″ × 34″, 1 square 5½″ × 5½″
- Red wool felt: 1 piece 10″ × 34″, 1 piece 1″ × 12″, 1 square 4″ × 4″
- ¼″-wide purple grosgrain ribbon: ⅓ yard
- Precut purple felt flower embellishment
- 1¼″-diameter yellow button: 1
- Threads to match felt colors
- Rotary cutter with pinking blade

Instructions

See pages 12–16 for working with felt.

1. Layer and pin together the 10″ × 34″ pieces of red and purple felt, matching the edges. Measure and mark a 9″ × 33″ rectangle in the center of the layered pieces.

2. To make the tote flap, measure 10″ from one end of the marked rectangle, and draw a line across the felt. Mark a 2″ × ¼″ rectangle centered on the marked line. Stitch around the small rectangle; then continue stitching all the way around the flap on the marked line. Carefully cut a slit through both layers inside the small rectangle. This slit will be the buttonhole for the handle.

3. To make the handle, center and pin the grosgrain ribbon onto the 1″ × 12″ red felt strip, and stitch along both edges of the ribbon. Fold the strip into a loop, and pin the loop to the red side of the tote with the cut ends of the loop centered 1″ from the edge of the tote opposite the flap. Use a narrow zigzag stitch to stitch over the cut ends of the handle. Insert a writing pen or pencil between the handle and the tote to form a slight loop in the handle, and pin the handle to the marked line at the edge of the tote. Stitch all the way across the marked end of the rectangle, catching the handle in your stitching.

Measure, mark, and stitch around flap; create buttonhole.

Make handle/pen holder, and attach it to end of tote.

4. Use the heart pocket pattern below to make a template (refer to Making and Using Pattern Templates on page 12). Transfer all the markings to the template. Arrange the heart template diagonally on the red felt square, trace the outline, and transfer the markings. Cut out the heart with a pinking blade.

5. Stitch around the top of the heart from dot to dot. Center the button on the felt flower, and stitch through the holes in the button to attach it to the center of the heart.

6. To make the pocket, trim the edges of the purple square with a pinking blade. Pin the heart to the center of the purple square. Stitch around the lower heart from dot to dot. Stitch across the upper edge of the square, starting and stopping ¼″ from the edge.

7. Pin the pocket to the tote flap with the top of the pocket facing the fold. Stitch the pocket in place around the side and lower edges of the purple square, starting and ending at the point of the previously stitched line.

Stitch pocket onto flap.

8. To finish, fold the tote with the red side out, and insert the handle through the buttonhole. Match the outlines, and pin the layers together along both sides and the folded lower edge. Stitch along the marked lines and ½″ from the folded lower edge. Use a pinking blade to trim all the edges, except the folded lower edge, ¼″ from the stitching.

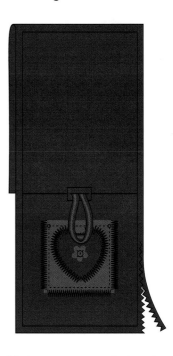

Stitch tote seams, and trim edges.

Heart pocket pattern

Here's an adorable, easy-to-make footstool featuring dimensional appliqués of felt flowers, hearts, and beads. This project starts with an inexpensive footstool (even more inexpensive if you can recycle a used footstool), which is covered with brightly colored wool felt and then embellished with decorative borders and motifs. You can adapt the design to fit a larger or smaller footstool by adjusting your measurements and materials. The materials listed below will cover the footstool shown, which is approximately 12″ square and 4″ high.

hearts and flowers footstool

Materials

See pages 7–11 for tools and materials.

- Footstool with detachable wooden bun feet: 12″ × 12″ × 4″

- Turquoise wool felt: 1 square 24″ × 24″, 4 pieces 2½″ × 11½″, 1 square 7½″ × 7½″

- Purple wool felt: 1 square 11½″ × 11½″, 1 square 8″ × 8″, and 4 pieces 3″ × 12″

- Green wool felt: 1 piece 9″ × 12″

- Orchid wool felt: 1 square 6″ × 6″

- Deep purple wool felt: 1 piece ½″ × 31″

- Yellow wool felt: 1 piece 2″ × 3″

- Size E lime green glass seed beads: 28

- Dimensional precut wool felt flowers 1″, in assorted bright colors: 24

- Dimensional precut wool felt hearts 1½″: 2 each red and hot pink, 4 lime green

- Wool felt mini-beads in assorted bright colors: 28

- Threads to match felt colors

- Staple gun

- Permanent fabric adhesive

- Sulky KK2000 repositionable adhesive spray

- Fabric marker: chalk, or air- or water-soluble marker

Instructions

See pages 12–16 for working with felt.

Cover the Footstool

1. Remove the feet, the fabric covering on the underside of the footstool, and any remaining staples or upholstery tacks. Note: If the previous covering is still smooth and clean, you can leave it in place. Otherwise, remove it carefully, and make sure that the foam or batting underneath is smooth and securely attached to the base.

2. Place the 24″ × 24″ square of turquoise felt on a smooth working surface. Center the footstool face down on the felt. Beginning at the center of each side, pull the felt smoothly around to the flat underside of the footstool, and staple the felt 1″ from the edge of the stool.

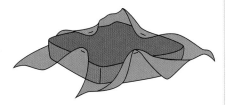

Staple felt to underside of footstool, working from centers of sides toward corners.

3. Smooth the felt at the corners, and trim away excess felt. Fold the remaining felt into a flat pleat, and staple diagonally across each corner to secure the fold. Trim away the remaining excess felt all the way around the footstool close to the staples.

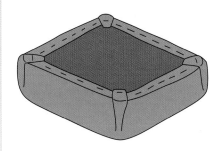

Pleat corners, and trim excess felt.

4. Arrange the 11½″ × 11½″ square of purple felt over the underside of the footstool so that all the staples are covered. Mark and cut holes in the felt where the feet will be attached.

5. Beginning from the center, use permanent fabric adhesive to attach the felt to the underside of the footstool.

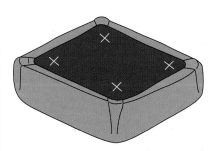

Glue felt to underside.

Make the Borders and Dimensional Appliqué

1. Use the patterns on the pattern pullout at the back of the book to make templates (refer to Making and Using Pattern Templates on page 12). Transfer all the markings to the templates.

2. To make the appliqué borders, apply temporary spray adhesive to 1 turquoise felt 2½″ × 11½″ strip, and adhere the strip to the center of 1 purple felt 3″ × 12″ strip. Stitch around the outer edges close to the edge of the turquoise felt. Repeat with the other 3 strips.

3. Transfer all markings from the templates onto the turquoise panels.

4. Trace and cut out 6 green felt leaves, 1 orchid felt flower, and 1 yellow felt flower center for each border panel. Cut the deep purple strip into 4 equal sections, and cut each into ⅛″-deep fringe.

Cut felt strips into fringe.

5. Using the template as your guide, arrange and pin the leaves onto each panel. Stitch around the edges and through the center of each leaf.

6. Arrange a flower in the center of each panel, and stitch around the outer edges of the flower. Mark the flower center, and stitch the fringe around the center mark. Stitch the flower centers in place, covering the edges of the fringe. Create a decorative spiral of stitches at the center of each flower.

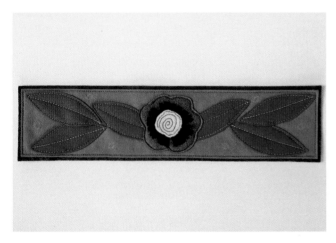

Stitch flower, fringe, and flower center to each border panel.

7. To assemble each dimensional flower, hand stitch a felt mini-bead, an E-bead, and a felt flower together. Make 24 flowers. Hand stitch or glue 6 flowers onto the marks on each border panel.

Hand stitch a felt bead and a glass bead onto each felt flower.

8. To make the footstool top panel, center the 7½″ × 7½″ turquoise felt square on the 8″ × 8″ purple square. Sew the turquoise square in place close to the edge.

9. Cut each of the dimensional lime felt hearts in half to create 2 leaf shapes. Referring to the photo, arrange a red or hot pink dimensional felt heart with 2 lime green leaf shapes in each corner of the turquoise felt square. Sew through the center of each shape to form the dimensional flower bud and leaves appliqué. Hand stitch a felt mini-bead topped with an E-bead onto each corner at the point where the leaves meet.

Stitch heart flower to top panel.

Assemble the Footstool

1. Attach the feet to the underside of the footstool.

2. Arrange the border panels with the ends meeting at the corners and the lower edges extending slightly over the lower edge of the footstool. Use permanent fabric adhesive to attach each border panel to the footstool.

3. Arrange the footstool top panel diagonally on the footstool with the 4 points centered and evenly spaced. Glue the panel in place.

Tranquil Bedroom—
Rose Garden Accents

Relax and unwind with these upscale accents and accessories designed to add a touch of tranquility to your personal retreat. The rich texture of felted wools combines with a counterpoint of sheer metallic organza to create a look of pampered elegance.

FINISHED PILLOW SIZE: 14″ × 19″

Relax and indulge with this soft muff-style pillow embellished with couched bouclé yarns and a flourish of sheer ruffle. The pistachio silk-lined interior provides a luxurious secret space to keep your private dream journal.

dream keeper pillow

Materials

See pages 7–11 for tools and materials.

- Washed and felted raspberry wool felt (refer to Fulling on page 14): 26″ × 36″

- Pistachio green silk crepe: 1 yard, 44″ wide

- Sheer metallic organza: 1¾ yard, 44″ wide

- Claret and pistachio bouclé novelty yarns: 6 yards of each color

- Threads to match felt and fabrics

- Metallic gold thread

- Thick upholstery batting: 1 piece 17″ × 30″

- Fabric marker: chalk, or air- or water-soluble marker

- Open-toe embroidery foot (optional)

Instructions

See pages 12–16 for working with felt.

1. Cut 1 rectangle 20″ × 30″ from the raspberry wool felt, cutting away the outer uneven edges. Cut 1 rectangle 20″ × 30″ from the pistachio green silk crepe. Cut 2 rectangles, each 4″ × 60″ from the sheer metallic organza.

2. To mark the couched yarn placement lines, mark the center of the raspberry rectangle. Measure 7/8″ on each side of the center and mark lines parallel to the long edges. Continue marking lines at 1¾″ intervals until you reach the edges. Use a wide, long zigzag stitch and metallic gold thread to couch the bouclé yarns onto the felt, alternating claret and pistachio stripes. Leave at least 2″ of felt unstitched at the outer edges to accommodate the seam allowances. Fold the felt in half widthwise with right sides together, matching the yarn stripes, and stitch into a tube using a ½″ seam allowance.

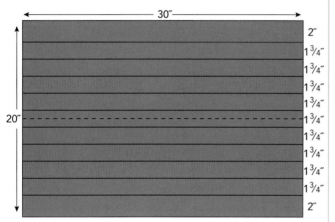

Mark lines for couching.

Couch yarn onto felted wool in stripes of alternating colors.

3. To make a ruffle strip for each end of the pillow, stitch together the short ends of an organza strip to form a loop. Fold each loop in half lengthwise, matching the long raw edges, and pin the open edges together. Stitch a double row of gathering stitches along the raw edges. Pull the threads to gather each loop to fit the tube.

4. Pin the ruffles to the open ends of the raspberry felt tube, matching the seams, and stitch.

Make ruffles, and stitch to felt tube.

5. Turn the ruffle out with the seam allowances to the inside of the tube and press.

6. On each end of the pillow, couch yarn onto the remaining marked line. Couch a final row of yarn to each end by stitching it in-the-ditch between the ruffle and the felt tube.

Couch yarn stripes between ruffles and felt tube.

7. Stitch the short ends of the silk crepe piece right sides together using a ½″ seam allowance to form a lining for the felt tube.

8. Turn under ½″ on both edges of the lining, and press wrong sides together at one end, matching the seams. Stitch through all the layers. Handstitch the lining in place.

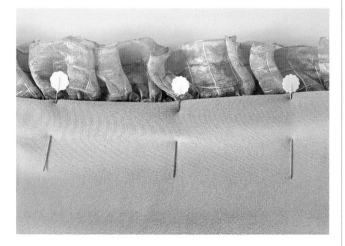

Pin felt and lining together at one end and handstitch together.

9. Roll the batting into a tube, and hand stitch the short ends together.

Hand stitch batting into tube.

10. Pull the felt layer over the batting.

Pull felt tube over batting.

11. Pull the lining firmly though the center of the batting tube, matching the seams. Pin the turned-under edge of the lining to the ruffle. Hand stitch the lining in place.

Hand stitch lining to ruffle.

FINISHED JOURNAL COVER SIZE: 8½″ × 11″

Created from several layers of wool felt, this stylishly simple journal cover is just the thing for keeping a record of your thoughts close at hand but under wraps. A few lines of straight stitches and cleverly placed cuts transform an ordinary blank book into a volume worthy of your most lofty hopes and dreams.

dream journal cover

Materials

See pages 7–11 for tools and materials.

- Hard-cover blank book with 8½″ × 11″ pages

- Raspberry and grass green wool felt: 1 piece 20″ × 27″ of each color

- ½″-diameter felt beads: 2 each purple and lime

- Threads to match felt colors

- Embroidery needle with large eye

- Chalk fabric marker

Instructions

See pages 12–16 for working with felt.

1. To make the bookmarks, cut 1 strip ⅝″ × 20″ of each felt color. Cut one end of each strip into a point. For each strip, thread the pointed end through the eye of the embroidery needle, and string on 2 beads.

2. Cut each color of the remaining felt into 2 rectangles 13″ × 20″. Layer the felt rectangles in alternating colors, starting with grass green on top. Measure and mark an 18¼″ × 11¾″ rectangle in the center of the top layer. Mark the center of one long side, and insert the square ends of the bookmarks between the layers until bookmarks extend inside the marked outline. Pin to secure. Stitch around the marked outline, being careful to catch the bookmarks in the seam.

Mark outlines. Insert bookmarks.

4. Make an opening to insert the journal cover by cutting away the green layer: cut on the cutting line, and just inside the stitching lines as shown below.

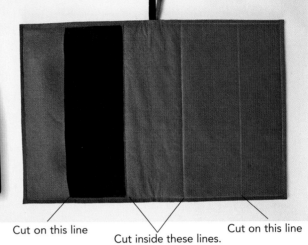

Cut on this line   Cut on this line

Cut inside these lines.

Cut away green layer to make pockets.

5. Turn the cover over. On the raspberry side, cut through one layer closely inside all the stitching lines, leaving the center spine area intact.

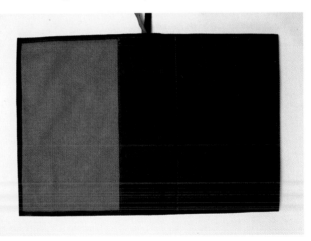

Cut away raspberry layer close to stitching lines.

3. Measure and mark cutting lines from top to bottom 3″ in from the outside stitching lines. Measure and mark stitching lines 4″ in from the cutting lines. Stitch along the stitching lines through all thicknesses. Trim the outer edges to ¼″ from the outside stitching line, being careful not to cut through the bookmarks.

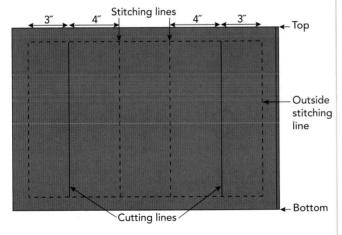

Measure and mark vertical lines. Stitch 2 inner lines.

6. Insert the front and back covers of the blank book into the pockets so the bookmarks are positioned from top to bottom. Arrange the bookmarks between the pages.

FINISHED STILL LIFE SIZE: 4½″ × 5½″

From across the room you might mistake this tiny framed still life for an impressionist painting. Closer examination, however, reveals the texture and dimension of the needle-felted surface. Wool roving and textured yarns combine to create a composition worthy of the opulent gold frame that completes your masterpiece.

still life with roses

Materials

See pages 7–11 for tools and materials.

- Purchased or recycled gold frame with 4″ × 5″ opening, glass not needed

- Cardboard cut to fit snugly inside frame

- Pistachio green wool felt: 1 piece 4½″ × 5½″

- Claret bouclé novelty yarn: 3 yards

- Brown yarn: ¾ yard

- Gold bouclé novelty yarn: small scraps

- Pink, wine, green, gold, and white wool roving: small amounts of each color

- Double-sided adhesive tape, or spray adhesive

- Fabric marker: chalk, or air- or water-soluble marker

- Felting needle and pad, or needle-felting machine

Instructions

See pages 12–16 for working with felt.

1. Trace the Still Life with Roses pattern on page 72, and transfer it onto the pistachio green felt (refer to Transferring Detail Lines on page 12).

2. Using the photo as your guide, needle felt the pink and wine roving onto the background to create the table and shadow. Needle felt the gold roving onto the vase shape, and add the white roving, blending it with the gold roving to create highlights on the vase as shown.

Needle felt roving onto felt background.

3. Needle felt the brown yarn in place over the transferred lines to create the stems.

Needle felt brown yarn onto felt background lines to create stems.

4. Using the photo as a guide, needle felt small bits of green roving along the stems to create the leaves. Note that a few of the leaves are felted over the stems and the front of the vase to create dimension.

Needle felt green roving along stems to create leaves.

5. Needle felt the claret bouclé yarn in circular patterns over the leaves and stems to create the flowers and buds. Begin at the center of each flower or bud, and wind the yarn around as you needle felt it in place. Add the gold yarn to the centers of the largest flowers.

6. Trim off any uneven outer edges, and attach the needle-felted picture permanently to the cardboard using double-sided adhesive tape or spray adhesive. Insert the finished piece into the frame.

Needle felt claret and gold yarns in circular patterns to create flowers.

Still Life with Roses pattern

FINISHED BED SCARF SIZE: 19″ × 59″

Add a touch of sheer opulence to your bedroom with this beautifully embellished organza end-of-the-bed coverlet featuring needle-felted dimensional rose appliqués. Elegant decorative end panels pay homage to antique tapestry patterns while celebrating contemporary upscale design with updated motifs and colors. Our model fits a double bed. Adjust the organza yardage for larger beds.

bed of roses sheer bed scarf

Materials

See pages 7–11 for tools and materials.

Note: yardage amounts are based on 36″-wide felt.

- Raspberry wool felt: ¾ yard
- Meadow green wool felt: ¼ yard
- Sheer gold metallic organza: 1¾ yards 44″ wide
- Claret and pink bouclé novelty yarns: 2 skeins of each color
- Pistachio bouclé novelty yarn: 1 skein
- Yellow bouclé novelty yarn: 5 yards
- Threads to match felt colors
- Metallic gold thread
- Fabric marker: chalk, or air- or water-soluble marker
- Felting needle and pad, or needle-felting machine

Instructions

See pages 12–16 for working with felt.

1. Use the patterns on the pattern pullout at the back of the book to make templates (refer to Making and Using Pattern Templates on page 12). Transfer all the markings to the templates.

2. Trace the end panel template twice onto raspberry felt, and cut out the pieces.

3. Pin the felt end panel pieces onto a single layer of the gold organza, and stitch close to the edges. Cut out the 2 panels close to the stitching.

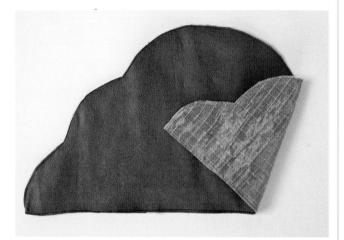

Pin panels onto organza, and stitch close to edges.

4. Trace the roses and rosebud templates onto the organza side of the panels. Mark the leaf placement.

Trace large and small roses and rosebud templates onto panels.

5. Needle felt yellow bouclé yarn to the center of each flower, wrapping the yarn in a circular motion. Begin at the yellow center, and needle felt the remaining area of each flower with pink bouclé yarn, applying the yarn in a circular pattern to cover the flower. Use a needle-felting machine for quick results.

6. Use a single hand-felting needle to add claret bouclé yarn outlines to the flower centers and rose petals.

Needle felt flower centers and petals onto panels.

7. Trace and cut out 41 leaf shapes from the meadow green felt. Use your fingers to pull the leaves lengthwise along the edges to stretch and ruffle the leaf edges.

Stretch leaves between fingers to ruffle edges.

8. Trim some of the felt leaves to fit around the curves of the rose petals, and arrange 14 leaves on each end panel. Needle felt through the center of each leaf with pistachio bouclé yarn to attach them. Leave the outer ruffled edges of the leaves free to add dimension.

9. Cut 1 organza rectangle 19″ × 60″. Clean finish the long edges with a narrow zigzag stitch. Use a long, wide zigzag stitch to couch claret and pistachio bouclé yarns along both finished edges. Use the same method to couch claret and pistachio yarns along the scalloped edge of each end panel.

10. With the organza rectangle wrong side up, pin an end panel right side down on each end of the rectangle, matching the straight edges. Stitch the straight edges together using a ½″ seam allowance; trim the seam allowances to ¼″. Turn the organza rectangle right side up, and fold the end panels right side up over the ends, encasing the seam; tuck any loose yarn ends inside the fold. Pin the end panels to the organza. Stitch the scalloped edges of the end panels in place, stitching between the couched claret and pistachio yarns.

Attach end panels to scarf at both ends.

11. Trace the medium rose template 7 times onto rose felt. Needle felt yellow bouclé yarn onto the flower centers. Needle felt claret yarn onto the petal outlines. Cut out the flowers close to the outline on the outer edge.

Trace medium rose template onto felt, and needle felt outlines and flower centers.

12. Referring to the photo, randomly arrange the flowers and leaves on the organza. Position the leaves under the flowers with the leaf tips meeting under the flower centers, and pin the leaves and flowers together. To attach each flower and its leaves securely to the scarf, stitch a small invisible circle of straight stitches around the flower center.

Arrange roses and leaves on scarf, and hand stitch in place around rose centers.

FINISHED TIEBACK SIZE: 3½″ × 26″

Here's a great way to add a touch of color and texture to coordinate a pair of plain sheer organza curtains with the other decorative elements in your bedroom. This project combines needle felting, reverse appliqué, and couched yarn techniques to create the look of simple opulence.

rose garden curtain tiebacks

Materials

See pages 7–11 for tools and materials.

- Washed and felted raspberry wool felt: 1 piece 19″ × 48″

- Moss green wool felt: 2 pieces 5″ × 22″

- Claret, gold, and pistachio bouclé novelty yarns: 6 yards of each color

- Threads to match felt colors

- Fabric marker: chalk, or air- or water-soluble marker

- Felting needle and pad, or needle-felting machine

Instructions

See pages 12–16 for working with felt.

1. Trim the outer uneven edges from the raspberry felt. Cut 2 strips 3″ × 45″ and 2 pieces 5″ × 22″.

2. Use the tieback pattern on the pattern pullout at the back of the book to make a template (refer to Making and Using Pattern Templates on page 12). Transfer all the markings to the template.

3. Trace the tieback template onto each piece of moss green felt. Transfer all the markings to the felt. With the marked side up, pin each green felt piece onto a matching raspberry felt piece, and stitch along the marked lines.

Stitch along all marked lines.

4. Cut out the tiebacks close to the stitched outlines. Use sharp-pointed scissors to trim away the moss green felt layer close to the stitching between the leaf shapes.

5. Needle felt the pistachio bouclé yarn in a continuous line through the centers of the leaves. Needle felt gold bouclé yarn in a circular pattern in the center of each flower. Needle felt claret bouclé yarn in a circular pattern around each flower center to cover the flower.

Needle felt yarn to create leaf veins and flowers.

6. Beginning with one long edge, roll up each of the 3″ strips of raspberry felt to create a 1″ × 45″-diameter cord. Press each cord lightly to flatten, centering the raw edge on one side. Bring the ends of the cord together, and hand stitch invisibly to form a continuous loop. With the raw edge centered on top, use a wide, long zigzag stitch to couch claret and pistachio bouclé yarns over the raw edge, stitching through all the layers of the flattened cord.

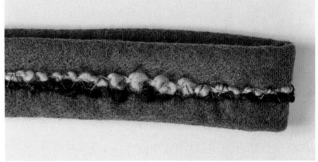

Couch yarns onto felt cord loop.

7. With the couched yarns facing up, pin each cord around the outer edges of a tieback with an equal loop of cord extending beyond each end of the tieback. Hand stitch the cord to the tieback, stitching around the outer edges of the tieback on the underside.

Stitch cord to tieback, creating loops at both ends.

8. To tie back your curtains, attach a small hook or nail at the edge of the window. Gather the curtain into the tieback and slide one loop through the other before hooking to the nail or hook.

sources

LYNNE FARRIS DESIGNS
Felting tools, kits, books, and supplies
1101 Juniper Street #404
Atlanta, GA 30309
www.lynnefarrisdesigns.com

C&T PUBLISHING, INC.
fast2fuse and Simply Stems
P.O. Box 1456
Lafayette, CA 94549
(800) 284-1114
ctinfo@ctpub.com
www.ctpub.com

CLOVER NEEDLECRAFT, INC.
Needle-felting tool and pad
13438 Alondra Boulevard
Cerritos, California 90703-2315
(800) 233-1703
www.clover-usa.com

ARTGIRLZ
Felt beads, precut flowers and hearts, and other fabulous stuff
4537B Old Post Road
Charlestown, RI 02813
(866) 507-4822
www.artgirlz.com

WEEKS DYE WORKS
Hand-dyed felted wools and fibers (wholesale only)
1510-103 Mechanical Boulevard
Garner, NC 27529
(877) OVERDYE
www.weeksdyeworks.com

BABY LOCK
Embellisher machine
www.babylock.com

NATIONAL NONWOVENS, INC.
Wool felt and needle-felting supplies (wholesale only)
P.O. Box 150
Easthampton, MA 01027
(800) 333-3469
www.nationalnonwovens.com

OGIER TRADING COMPANY
Hand-dyed yarns and fibers (wholesale only)
P.O. Box 686
Moss Beach, CA 94038
(800) 637-3207

YLI CORPORATION
Silk hankies and novelty threads
1439 Dave Lyle Boulevard
Rock Hill, SC 29730
(803) 985-3100
www.ylicorp.com

JUNE TAILOR, INC.
Fancy Fleece Ruler
P.O. Box 208
2861 Hwy 175
Richfield, WI 53076
(800) 844-5400
www.junetailor.com

THERM O WEB
SuperTape double-sided adhesive
770 Glenn Avenue
Wheeling, IL 60090
(800) 323-0799
www.thermoweb.com
Available at major craft stores

BEACON ADHESIVES, INC
Fabri-Tac and Felt Glue
125 MacQuesten Parkway South
Mount Vernon, NY 10550
(914) 699-3405
www.beaconcreates.com

SULKY OF AMERICA
KK2000 spray adhesive
980 Cobb Place Boulevard
Suite 130
Kennesaw, GA 30144
(800) 874-4115
www.sulky.com

For a list of other fine books from C&T Publishing, ask for a free catalog:
C&T PUBLISHING, INC.
P.O. Box 1456
Lafayette, CA 94549
(800) 284-1114
ctinfo@ctpub.com
www.ctpub.com

C&T Publishing's professional photography services are now available to the public. Visit us at www.ctmediaservices.com.

For quilting supplies:

COTTON PATCH
1025 Brown Ave.
Lafayette, CA 94549
Store: (925) 284-1177
Mail order: (925) 283-7883
CottonPa@aol.com
www.quiltusa.com

about the author

Lynne Farris brings a lifetime of design experience to the world of creative sewing and fiber arts.

Trained as a visual artist, she earned master of fine arts degree in painting before beginning her career as a college art instructor. She worked for several years as a designer in the toy and juvenile products industries and has had her own business since 1982 as a designer of puppets, corporate and sports mascots, and props for commercials.

Lynne is the author of six books on fiber arts, including *Fresh Felt Flowers* and *Fast, Fun & Easy Needle Felting*, published by C&T Publishing. She appears frequently on HGTV, DIY, and PBS as a guest on creative programs.

She shares her expertise as a creative consultant to several leading manufacturers and is the owner of Lynne Farris Gallery in Atlanta, Georgia, where many of her textile works are on display.

Photo by Sonny

OTHER BOOKS BY LYNNE FARRIS

To learn more about Lynne, visit her website at www.lynnefarrisdesigns.com

Great Titles
from C&T PUBLISHING

table toppers
OhSewEasy
27 Projects for Stylish Living
Jean & Valori Wells

your space
my make it you
Sew with Style Easy Step-by-Step Instructions Uniquely You
Shannon Mullen

life style
OhSewEasy
20 Projects to Make Your Home Your Own
Valori Wells & Carolyn Spencer

Embellishing with Felted Wool
16 Projects with Appliqué, Beads, Buttons & Embroidery
MARY STORI

Fleece Dog
A little bit of magic created with raw wool and a special needle
SINCO

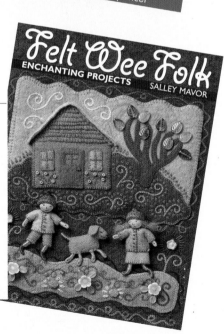

Felt Wee Folk
ENCHANTING PROJECTS SALLEY MAVOR